Reinventing my World

Life After Stroke

Reinventing my World

Life After Stroke

Joslien Wannechko

REINVENTING MY WORLD
Life After Stroke

Copyright © 2022, Joslien Wannechko.

All rights reserved. No part of this publication may be reproduced, stored in a retrieval system, or transmitted in any form or by any means, electronic, mechanical, photocopying, recording, or otherwise, without written permission of the author and publisher.

Published by Joslien Wannechko, Ryley, Alberta, Canada

ISBN
Paperback: 978-1-77354-393-2
ebook: 978-1-77354-395-6

Publication assistance by

PUBLISHING
PageMaster.ca

Acknowledgements

I am very appreciative of my husband, Alvin. He has been there every step of the way. From staying nights with me when I first had the stroke to the constant care and support when I came home Alvin has been my rock.

My eldest son, Alvin (Gerald) and his wife Tammy constantly encouraged me. Gerald even bought an Apple iPad so we could communicate easily. He gave me instructions that I could call him anytime. He took it to work so he was available if I wished to speak with him. Having that family connection when I was not allowed more visitors meant the world to me.

My second son Lee was one of my designated visitors and he never missed a week-end until he began working twelve hours a day, six days a week. His warped sense of humor helped keep me going. Lee's daughter Kaylee Wannechko, her significant other Carson Orieux, and Lee's youngest daughter Adrianna Wannechko also visited me when I was in the hospital in Camrose. They lifted my spirits at a time when I really needed it.

My daughter Elaine (Laine) came when I needed her most. Thankfully borders were still open. We still communicate with Laine and her partner Pony through video chat weekly.

To my granddaughters Kaylee Wannechko, Samantha Wannechko-Harbin, and Tanya Wannechko as well as their significant others thank you for allowing me to teach when I was still on the road to recovery. You showed me I was able to speak long enough to teach a class like I did before the stroke. Another big thank you to Tanya and Kaylee for help in editing. It meant the world to me.

I would be remiss if I did not thank all the other people who helped me in proof reading and editing my manuscript. My dear friends and former neighbors Janet

Winsnes and Allison Fitt did the first edit. Thank you. Another thank you to my old friends Darlene Kozicky and Gloria Lecopoy. Your editing, support and encouragement in this endeavor mean a lot to me. When I say old, I mean we have been friends for about fifty years. They are still young at heart.

A special thank you to Aarani Suhapirmam, Michelle Dionne-Nesbitt and Tammy Wannechko. Your suggestions in editing were invaluable and so professional. Thanks also to Trina Orieux who did a final proofread before I sent it to the publisher. You all helped me present a finished professional product I was proud of.

A special thank you to Elizabeth Dupuis. The very next day after I told her what I wanted, she went out and took a beautiful picture of a sunrise for the cover of my book. You are indeed a gem!

As I've mentioned in the book, I am extremely grateful to all who supported and cared for me; nursing staff, therapists, and home care aides. I couldn't have done this without you.

Table of Contents

Chapter	Page. No.
1. The Beginning	1
2. Moving Forward	8
3. Gratitude	13
4. No One Wants Me	15
5. Glimmer of Light	17
6. Red Deer	22
7. Tofield	34
8. More Hard Work	40
9. Keep Going	45
10. And Still Keep Going	49
11. Little Victories	51
12. Light At The End Of The Tunnel	55
13. Brett's Story	58
14. Slow Changes	63
15. Family Perspective	66
16. Dawn Of A New Day	71

> *"The struggle you are in today is developing the strength you need for tomorrow. Don't give up."*
> Robert Tew

Chapter 1
The Beginning

There are a few signs and symptoms of a stroke that are taught by Red Cross, St. John Ambulance and the Heart and Stroke Foundation. The acronym FAST is often used when first aid classes are taught.

F Facial Droop Does one side of the face appear to droop? Is there any numbness or tingling on one side? Does their smile appear even?

A Arm Drift Can the person bring up both arms in front of the body, parallel to each other or does one arm refuse to lift or drift downwards?

S Speech Is the speech slurred? Does the person appear confused, perhaps searching for words or using the wrong words? Do they have a problem comprehending what someone else is saying?

T Time Time is of the essence. It is critical to get the affected person to a medical facility as quickly as possible to minimize damage.

There are many other symptoms which include sudden severe headache, dizziness, trouble walking, or a loss of balance and coordination.

March 2nd, 2020 started like any other. Little did I know the events that started that day would bring about a drastic change to my life. I was sitting in my favorite spot, a leather recliner with my feet elevated and my laptop on my knees. As I sat there playing solitaire, I became aware of my tongue feeling "funny". It was not numb, just fuzzy.

As a first aid instructor for the past 30 years, I was well aware of the signs and symptoms associated with a stroke. Immediately I rose and ran to the bathroom to look at myself in the mirror. The face that stared back at me appeared normal, no hint of a droop on either side. Since I had run to the bathroom, obviously there was no problem with coordination. My balance was not affected. Just to confirm, I held out both arms in front of me. Both of them remained steady. Breathing a sigh of relief, I returned to my comfortable chair.

The rest of the day continued uneventfully except for that "fuzzy" feeling in my tongue. I monitored my speech throughout the day and had no issues speaking clearly. After checking myself in the mirror again and still finding no signs of a stroke, it was time for bed. Perhaps I would get it checked out the next day. Perhaps this was a Transient Ischemic Attack (TIA). With a TIA, symptoms usually disappear within 24 hours. Since there had been no textbook symptoms, I was doubtful this was a TIA.

At approximately 2 a.m. I awoke. I was still very aware of the fuzzy tongue. Again, I went to the bathroom to check out my face. Just as before, there was no telltale droop and no arm drift. Still feeling uneasy I woke my husband Alvin and told him I felt I needed to go to the hospital. "Should we call an ambulance or can I drive you?" he questioned.

"An ambulance!" I responded. Not wanting to be caught in a state of undress, I proceeded to don joggers while my husband called 911. In a period of about five minutes a strange thing happened. I wanted to go around to the side of the bed. Although I could stand, my feet would not move! I sat down, then laid on the bed. When the 911 operator asked my husband our gate address and I tried to tell my husband what it was, no sound came out. I used my fingers to sign the numbers at the gate. My left hand would not work at all, only my right hand was able to move slightly. My mind was totally clear; it was my body that would not do what I wanted it to. A sense of frustration built, it felt as if I was no longer in control. Thank goodness I was lying on the bed. Within a few minutes I was unable to stand.

When the ambulance arrived, the stretcher was used to transport me to the ambulance. Then we proceeded to the hospital which was forty-five minutes away. EMS personnel suggested Camrose hospital was better equipped to handle strokes.

By now it was evident that I had suffered a stroke. I have since learned that ambulances are directed to go to the nearest hospital which has the capability of performing CT scans.

In Camrose, when Alvin and I were asked when the symptoms started, I was in a bit of a quandary. My symptoms had started the afternoon before but had not gotten critical until about 2 hours previously. I was unable to speak to clarify. I am still not completely sure if perhaps the medical team administered the drug, Tissue Plasminogen Activator (TPA) which is a clot buster, the effects would have been this severe. There is only a short window of time, three or four hours after a stroke, that this drug can be administered. Nursing staff felt the window had passed. Unknown to me they told my husband, and later my son, that it could cause bleeding if it was administered later. I was just aware the drug had not been given and I was afraid I would not regain the use of my voice and limbs.

The next few hours were pretty much a blur. I never lost consciousness and I was always aware. It was comforting to have nursing staff nearby. I was given a CT scan and then later another. At one point in time, I was asked to stand to transfer into a chair. I collapsed. My legs could not bear my weight. Slowly, I was beginning to partially understand the enormity of my situation.

To my surprise, my son Lee came in to see me instead of going to work. My eldest son Alvin Jr. and his wife Tammy were the next to arrive. I still did not understand why they felt it necessary to miss work and come and see me. Much, much later, months in fact, my husband admitted that they did not expect me to survive.

What made this whole situation bearable is the next day Lee told me about an experience a co-worker had related to him. His father had a severe stroke and a year later he was walking. This gave me hope and my mind would return to this story many times especially in darker days.

The day after the stroke, my writing was much like it had been pre-stroke. But, later that day, I felt as if I regressed. I could barely lift my right hand. Writing was difficult. The nurse assured me nothing was wrong. I still felt uneasy. Several months later I learned I had a TIA (mini stroke) that day. I guess she thought I did not need to know. My writing did not improve to its previous level, but it did get somewhat better. I wonder, would I have felt better if she confirmed what I already knew and then reassured me I would be okay? I don't know. I did, however, know something was wrong. Although the writing itself was not my main concern it showed me my condition had deteriorated. The fact that my writing did improve slightly in a few days was a tiny bit of comfort but what was more important I could once more raise my right hand a few inches.

A few days after my stroke, my daughter Elaine (Laine) who lives in Lexington, Kentucky flew in to see me. I was overjoyed. She was starting a new job the following week, so, thankfully she had a few days off. She was only able to stay for three or four days, which was fortunate because borders were closed a week or two later due to Covid 19. She flew home just in time.

My entire family stayed positive when they saw me. No one even hinted I would not be able to do the things I thought I might be able to. Many months later, my oldest son admitted he was only hoping I would be able to get enough movement in my right hand to be able to play on the computer. Thankfully he kept his fears to himself. Knowing that my family felt I would not make a full recovery would have been devastating.

As the days wore on, reality reared its head. I had to be fed through a tube, and after a week or so, I had a tube called a peg put directly into my stomach. I could not tolerate the food and vomited constantly. One doctor explained that my stomach was paralysed. A second procedure was done to push the tube in further. This failed to help as the tube folded back on itself. And yet another operation, this time to place the tube into the jejunum, which is attached on one end to the small intestine and on the other to the duodenum, which is attached to the pyloric valve at the end of the stomach.

Each time there was an operation I made sure the doctor was aware I had a Do Not Resuscitate (DNR) order. By this time, it appeared I might be confined to bed or propped in a chair for the rest of my life. So, if there was a chance I could die on the operating table, I did not want them to revive me just so I could spend the rest of my days totally dependent on others. With the first operation I was a bit hesitant about the DNR order; by the third, I was disappointed that I awoke from the anaesthetic. The idea of staying alive and being bedridden and incapacitated filled me with dread. The thought of laying in bed twenty-four hours a day and being tended to like a baby was not something I contemplated with any degree of enthusiasm.

    I had even written a message to my family saying good-bye. I often told Alvin I loved him but saying it one more time might bring him a bit of comfort. I knew Alvin Jr. had a loving and supportive spouse and she and their grown daughters would assist him in dealing with his grief. The same was true for my daughter Laine. Her partner Pony would support her and provide comfort. I was the most concerned with my son Lee. He was divorced and only had his girls, who although they loved him dearly did not live with him. Although I knew he would be there for his dad, I wanted to remind him his dad was still there for him as well. My family meant the world to me and I wanted them to know how much I loved and appreciated them. I knew they were aware of how much I cared but being told one last time might help them a tiny bit especially during the initial stages of the grieving process. I was not afraid of dying, my concern was for my family I was leaving behind.

    Another avenue I explored was Medical Assistance In Dying (MAID). However, in order to qualify there must be an estimated anticipated date of death. In my case there was none. I could live for years in this condition. So, this was another dead end. The thought of being bedridden was incomprehensible. There is now talk of those who are totally incapacitated being eligible for MAID. Personally, I am still an advocate for MAID with perhaps a longer evaluation period. I did not begin to get noticeably better until three months after my stroke.

"Small steps in the right direction can turn out to be the biggest step of your life."
Good Housekeeping

Chapter 2
Moving Forward

All this time my communication was limited to spelling out words by pointing to the alphabet written on a paper. I used this method of conversing with others for nearly three months since I could not speak. A few weeks after my stroke, I worked with a speech therapist who started me on my journey of regaining my voice. One doctor suggested I get a tablet which had a program that could help me communicate. My husband's brother-in-law brought in one of his with a program installed. I did attempt to use it, but it took a great deal of effort to figure it out and remember where everything was. The stroke did not affect my memory, I don't think; it's just that I have never been computer savvy. When I am learning something new, I need to make notes and write everything down. I decided to just use my way of pointing to letters and spelling out words. For myself, this was easier.

Then the Corona Virus (Covid 19) made its devastating appearance. We heard about it on the news, but it was mostly affecting people in China and other locations far from Canada. But before we knew it, it was in our faces. Alvin was staying overnight with me at the hospital. Since I could not speak, I depended on him to tell the nurses what I needed. It was easier to communicate with him; he seemed to know instinctively what I needed. I guess this is the result of being together for nearly fifty years.

First, he was told he could not stay overnight. Then a week later he was told he could not see me at all. I was heart-broken. He was my rock and my anchor. Since he had a forty-five-minute drive to come see me, nursing staff called him and gave him the news so he would not make the trip in for nothing. Not being able to see him left a huge hole in my day. I felt so utterly alone. Thankfully the nursing staff were very kind, caring and supportive. They took their time when attending to me. There was one particular nurse who deserves recognition. She was not one of my regular care-givers; she was working when I first came in and her regular duties were with the heart and stroke unit. This angel brought in a home-made quilt for me to use on my bed. The bright colors added a slash of cheer to the hospital décor. Even today whenever I use the quilt, it brings me a sense of joy. I will always remember her smiling eyes and the dark hair that framed her face.

My inability to swallow and constant saliva caused me to drool constantly. Thankfully I was able to manoeuvre my right arm enough to use a suction. I was grateful to be able to deal with this ongoing issue by myself. I continued to require this suction for five to six months.

Then small changes began to happen. I stayed at St. Mary's Hospital in Camrose for nearly three months. During that time, I continued Speech Therapy. I made progress by beginning to say a few phrases. My voice was barely above a whisper. But at least it was a start.

Physical therapy was also on the agenda. There was a Therapy Assistant who came every day. Each day she massaged my left hand which did not move at all. I think my mental health derived as much benefit from her visits as my left hand did. During this time, I also went to the Physiotherapy Department. I spent most of the time sitting in the wheelchair stacking cones; it was an activity that was used to strengthen my hand. I forced my right hand to keep trying to move the cones into different piles. Focusing on coordination as well as lifting the cones which weighed only a few ounces required a great deal of effort. My crowning achievement however was sitting for two minutes unaided on the plinth. A plinth is a large padded "table" used in the physical therapy department.

There was one major problem. The dietician and I were at odds. First, she had me on a diabetic formula for the tube feed. The diabetic formula was high in protein and lower in carbohydrates. Then it was changed to a regular formula which had more carbohydrates, which in turn helped elevate blood glucose levels. When I mentioned my concern about the regular formula to the doctor, he said the dietitian was unable to obtain the diabetic one. However, I overheard a conversation with a nurse and apparently the diabetic formula took more effort to obtain, but it was not impossible. My overall impression of the dietician took a downward spiral.

She did try to do things by the book and according to her standards, I was to have a certain amount of "food." However, my stomach would not tolerate it and I continuously vomited. Thankfully, a kind nurse told me that it was up to me if I wished to refuse treatment. I am not sure why I did not think of this myself. Maybe, because instead of questioning like I usually did, I just assumed the medical profession knew more than I did. Before this, I had only very limited experience with anyone who had had a stroke.

The dietitian lowered the amount of food I took but she increased the amount of water. The result was the same as before. I began vomiting again. This time there was no hesitation. I refused to take the increased water and my vomiting subsided. I did not have any more conversations with the dietitian. She accepted that I had control of how much nourishment I allowed into my body. My body was able to tolerate the limited amount of "food" and water I was now given.

Even with the visiting restrictions in place, I was able to circumvent them. A few weeks after the restrictions took effect, I asked the nurses to wheel me outside. My husband and son were in the parking lot as we had previously arranged on the phone. One time Lee brought his daughters, Adrianna and Kaylee. Kaylee was accompanied by a person who was very special to her. I didn't hug them, but it lifted my spirits just seeing all of them. We took precautions, used masks, and also practised social distancing. My husband did not go anywhere except for home and the hospital. Lee was screened every day at work. We all felt we were doing a good job of being safe. Seeing my husband and son meant the world to me. At this time seniors in long term care facilities were not allowed visitors at all. I counted my blessings that I had these few, brief visits when so many others in seniors' long term care centres were locked up as if in jail! Their doors may not have been physically locked, but they were not allowed to congregate together or have any visitors.

Apparently, the stroke was in my brain stem. Both sides of my body were affected, which is why there had been no facial droop. My left hand was unable to move at all, and my right had very limited movement. As instructors of first aid, we are taught the classical symptoms, not the variations of which there are many.

In possibly a month after the stroke I was sent for a swallow test to the Red Deer Hospital. This test consists of fluids and food that was of pudding-like consistency mixed with barium. What vile tasting food this was! The objective of the swallow test was to see if liquids or food would go down the esophagus and into the stomach as they were meant to, or if they entered the airway and went down into the lungs. If food or water gets into the lungs, aspiration pneumonia may result. The feeding tube would prevent this from happening.

The results were disheartening. I was not allowed to drink or eat. All my nourishment came through the feeding tube. I returned to the Camrose Hospital in low spirits. One of my doctors tried to reassure me that I could eventually go home even with a feeding tube. I did know this was possible since our neighbour had one for many months while he convalesced at home before he passed away from cancer. However, going home with a feeding tube was not something I contemplated with any degree of enthusiasm.

In order to transfer me from the bed to the wheelchair, a sling was used. The nurses would roll me on one side, place the sling under me, then roll me to the other side and finish positioning it in place. Then a mechanical lift called a Hoyer lifted me up into the air and transferred me into my wheelchair or back into bed. Thus, I was transferred safely. This would continue for five months, until August in fact.

*"Acknowledging the good you already have in your life
is the foundation for all abundance."*
Eckhart Tolle

Chapter 3
Gratitude

Progress was slow but at least there was progress. The upside was that although both sides of my body were affected, my right side did begin to recover; very slowly, ever so slowly, but it did happen.

I have always believed that everything happens for a reason. I still do not understand why my stroke occurred. The medical explanation is that it was caused by atrial fibrillation. This is the irregular beating of the atrium or upper chamber of the heart. The blood pools and becomes sluggish which may result in blood clots. If the clot travels to the brain it can result in a stroke.

I understand the medical perspective, however in my pursuit of personal growth I have learned everything happens for a reason. The body is much more than just a physical entity. Mental, emotional, and spiritual elements come into it. I tried to look at my situation dispassionately. Did this happen because I no longer wanted to work and subconsciously wanted a way out? I didn't think so because I had already made the decision to stop teaching first aid in the coming year. I knew I would not be renewing my instructor status in 2022. Or was I wanting validation that my family cared? They definitely were there showing their support for me. Perhaps I may never completely know the why, but I do know I can be a good example of persevering when the odds seem insurmountable. And perhaps I did not have to understand the why; what was necessary was the determination to move forward, one step at a time.

One of my beliefs is that we need to practise gratitude. The more grateful we are, the more that good comes our way. Every day, even in the early part of the stroke, I expressed my thanks to the staff for their assistance, regardless if they were changing my drawers or getting me a tissue. Although I did it with no thought of reward, I reaped many benefits. The staff were exceptional. I cannot say enough good things about them. If I was feeling a bit down, they often shared personal tidbits with me. This had an uplifting effect and showed me how very lucky I was. I will not share these stories as they were of a personal nature, and I feel it would be betraying a confidence.

One nurse cut my hair. It had grown a bit longer than I normally had it due to Covid and then being bedridden because of the stroke so I really appreciated her efforts. She did a great job.

One exceptional nurse helped me get ready for a "date" with my husband. She helped me with my hair, my make-up; all to visit with my husband in the parking lot. The make-up was not mine; she brought some mascara for me as well as the lipstick. What a gem she was! She definitely went above and beyond in her duties. I felt Camrose had the very best staff and from the bottom of my heart I thank them.

Gratitude did not mean everything always went smoothly. For example, I did have to stand up for myself with the dietician and once with nursing staff, but the outcomes were always positive.

"Gratitude and attitude are not challenges; they are choices."
Robert Braathe

Chapter 4
No One Wants Me

Finally, it was time to leave the Camrose hospital and go to a Rehab Program. Since my doctor felt I would benefit from some intense rehabilitation, applications were sent to the Glenrose in Edmonton, Sage Stroke and Geriatric Unit in Two Hills and Red Deer Rehabilitation Unit.

A few weeks later, we received some replies. The Glenrose, which is apparently a great rehab center would not take me since I was on a continuous tube feed. I did not meet their criteria because there were no gaps between my meals which would make working with therapists difficult.

Two Hills felt they would not be able to help me very much. I had looked forward to going there since it was only an hour from home. Ponoka, which is where the rehab patients from Red Deer were, also felt I would not be a good candidate. I couldn't believe it. No one wanted to give me a chance. If I did not go to rehab, I might not have a choice but go into a long-term care facility. I simply required more care than my husband was capable of doing, twenty-four hours a day, seven days a week. I was devastated. Thankfully, my doctor persevered and wrote a letter to Red Deer explaining my goals and asking them to give me an opportunity for some rehabilitation.

Originally, when I was asked what my goals were, they were simple. I wanted to walk. This time it was still the same. However, knowing the people in charge felt that goal was unachievable I gave them much simpler ones; going to the bathroom myself, brushing my hair etc. All the while in the back of my mind, I kept saying, "I'm going to walk!"

A couple of weeks later the doctor came with some news. Red Deer accepted me on a two-week trial basis. I was giddy with relief. Intuitively, I knew with rehabilitation therapy I would at least progress to the point of being able to go home where my husband would be able to look after me. I would be going to Ponoka which is where the Red Deer Rehabilitation Unit had been moved because of Covid. Part of me was sad and also a bit afraid. I was comfortable in Camrose. I liked the staff and they liked me. Who knew what the nursing staff were like in Ponoka! So, it was with some trepidation that I was taken by ambulance to Ponoka. I arrived in Ponoka the last week of May.

"You will face many defeats in life, never let yourself be defeated."
Maya Angelo

Chapter 5
Glimmer of Light

It was about this time I was given another swallow test. So back for another ambulance ride to Red Deer. Again, the vile tasting "food." It took a great deal of effort not to vomit. On the positive side, now I was able to eat pureed food! I still had the tube feed to make sure I had enough nourishment - but in my eyes, this was a giant step forward. This was about four months after my stroke. I was allowed to drink water. Oh, the joy I felt! What a treat! I returned to Ponoka in high spirits.

For my next meal I was escorted to a small dining area. It turned out only people who were in danger of choking ate here. I was ecstatic! I was eating and swallowing food. Some of it looked gross and didn't taste great, but it was my first step to eating real food! The suggestion was to eat 75% of my meal. I did not have a problem with that at all. One of the dishes that sticks out in my mind was a barley soup. Because it was pureed, it resembled gravy. The taste left a lot to be desired! I could not eat more than a couple mouthfuls. The rest of the meal which was probably meat, potatoes, and vegetables, was tolerable. There was a lady who was on a regular diet, who complained about the carrots. "They are horrible," she said, "obviously frozen." I remember thinking "Well at least you have real food, not this slop."

Ordinarily I was a social person and loved to talk. The largest obstacle to this was that my voice was hardly louder than a whisper. It was difficult for people to hear, let alone understand me. It was very frustrating to have people nod their heads as if in understanding but I could tell from their expressions or their responses that they had not understood. I learned to use gestures with a minimal amount of words. This was not as satisfactory to me as verbal communication, but least I did have some social interaction. On the upside, I had a private room again. If I would see someone in the hallway, I would wave them in and show off my window. I made two friends who I totally enjoyed. Both ladies were patients in their mid-eighties.

Then I met Carrie, my physical therapist. She was awesome but did not pull any punches. She said the chances of me walking were slim to none. When I was in my room later, I cried and cried. One of my new friends came and told me the doctor had said she would never walk. And lo and behold she was using a walker! I doubted this would happen because Carrie didn't believe I would. I believed the sun rose and set with Carrie!

On the first day with her, she had me use the sit-to-stand. It allows a person to stand by the use of counter weights to help pull you up. Carrie put on fifty-pound weights and I was able to stand for the first time in nearly three months. I could feel weight on my legs! You cannot understand how this feels unless you have been through a similar experience. We did this every day. After a few days, I realized the backs of my thighs were sore. I couldn't contain my feeling of glee and wonderment. I was strengthening my muscles. Once more, I had hope that I would walk again.

Five days a week, I had one hour of therapy with Carrie in the morning. In the afternoon there was an hour with an assistant, usually doing arm exercises.

Two weeks after I arrived in Ponoka there was a formal review of my progress. Carrie sensed my nervousness and reassured me that she would speak of my improvement and determination. I was somewhat relieved. However, not until the meeting was over and it was guaranteed I would be allowed to stay for at least another month did I completely relax. The specture of a nursing home no longer loomed as a possibility.

It was at the review where I met Dr. McLean, a physiatrist, via zoom. A physiatrist treats a wide variety of medical conditions affecting the brain, spinal cords, nerves, bones, joints, ligaments, muscles, and tendons. I have come to admire and respect her.

The first big hurdle was over! I knew there would be progress meetings every month, but if all it took was hard work, I knew I would be with them for a while. The therapy sessions were exhausting. Some days I did very well, then they were followed by days when I did poorly. This was a judgement on my part. Any time I was down on myself because I could not do things I had done previously, Carrie patiently reminded me the recovery cycle after a stroke is filled with ups and downs, with peaks and valleys. Looking back, I am surprised she didn't shake me and remind me she had already told me this. Through all my months at Ponoka and then Red Deer she kept encouraging me.

I have since learned that many stroke survivors have anger outbursts or resentments about what they lost because of the stroke. Although I sometimes felt I was not progressing fast enough I channeled all my energy into the therapy sessions.

I was so very pleasantly surprised as I got to know the nursing staff in Ponoka. They were even better or as good as Camrose. I want to thank each and everyone of them for how much they helped me.

One angel took me outside in my chair a few times. Once, we stopped to pick a handful of lilacs. This particular nurse also cut my hair again. I considered myself very lucky. Yes, I was in hospital for many months but during that time I had two haircuts, one in Camrose and one in Ponoka. Another angel took my pants home and washed and mended them. There will always be a special corner in my heart for them. They went above and beyond their duties.

Another bonus was the dietitian. I related my encounter in Camrose and was very relieved when I learned she would work with me for the best possible outcome for my treatment.

One day the Recreation Assistant took me outside for some fresh air. It was afternoon, the sun was shining; it was a glorious day. I had already had therapy which depleted my limited stamina. I remember sitting in my wheelchair, leaning to the right, with my right arm hanging down. I did not have the strength to sit up or lift my right arm to place it on the arm of the wheelchair. This was three to four months after the stroke. She took me back inside and helped me back into bed. Gratefully I accepted her help. In later months when I did not feel I was progressing I would think back to this incident to remind myself of how far I had come.

I stayed in Ponoka almost the entire month of June. With dedication, perseverance, and a lot of hard work along with Carrie's constant encouragement, I was able to progress on the sit stand without the use of any counterweights. This was exhilarating! I could stand! Not for long perhaps, and I had to hold onto the ropes, but this was a step forward nonetheless.

All during this time Alvin and Lee came to visit weekly. The province had new regulations in place. Each hospital patient was allowed the same two visitors. Alvin and Lee were mine. They usually came on Sunday which was awesome since I had no therapy on weekends. Ponoka was about a one and one-half hour drive each way for them.

Then came the day we would all be moving to Red Deer. There was a drop in the numbers for Covid 19 patients and the Rehab Unit was moving back home. Once more I was filled with trepidation. Yes, this staff was coming as well, but what about the new staff. It was a bigger unit and there would also be more patients. What if I didn't receive the same level of loving care? This may sound silly but remember I was pre-occupied with getting better. I was definitely grateful to the nursing staff but my primary focus was myself. That was my major concern.

I gave myself a mental slap. I had always believed gratitude was the key to getting what you wanted and I was extremely grateful to all the wonderful staff. Red Deer would be fine, I reminded myself.

"When we focus on gratitude, the tide of disappointment goes out and the tide of love rushes in."
Kristin Armstrong

Chapter 6
Red Deer

I was one of the second last patients to be transported to Red Deer. I was afraid I would be sharing a room with someone. Imagine my delighted surprise when I got a private room with a window. The Rehab Unit was on the third floor, but I did get a glimpse of a few trees in the parking lot and I would also get to see some hot air balloons.

My first encounter with nursing staff was less than ideal. I was still on a tube feed as well as my meals which were pureed. Since I arrived in the evening, I was taken straight to my room. My bed was always set at a thirty-degree incline to minimize the possibility of "food" entering my airway and going into my lungs. This nurse set the incline to forty-five degrees. It was very uncomfortable to try to sleep in this position. I asked the nurse to lower the incline, but she was adamant and I was unable to change the settings from my bed. When she left the room, I indulged in a few minutes of self pity then chose to focus on being grateful for the private room.

Thankfully one of my "angels" came on shift at eleven. She also made sure she wrote in the nursing notes that I used the thirty-degree incline. The next afternoon when the first nurse came back on shift, she immediately changed the incline back to forty-five. I told her to check the nursing notes and she did find I was correct. There was no hint of apology, but I was too happy and grateful to hold a grudge, well, at least not for long.

Meals were in the dining room. Only two people were allowed per table because of Covid.

I was so fortunate. I got to share a table with a man who I shall call Penthouse Paul, a gentleman in his mid-eighties. He shared a room, but the room was huge with windows on two sides. Hence, the name, Penthouse Paul.

Because my voice was very quiet, he became my intermediary. If I needed a nurse, Paul would get their attention. We played shuffleboard on our long table using a Kleenex box. Paul went home long before I did, and I was very happy for him but it did leave a small gap for a while. Before he left, he did give me a special gift although he did not realize it. He said, "Whenever Carrie asks me to do something, I do it plus one more." After that I tried to do the same, especially if I was doing bed exercises with Martina, the sweet, supportive therapy assistant. It is this type of attitude that has kept me going and brought me so far along.

Rehabilitation continued with no let up. Since I had mastered the sit-to-stand, I was now using an apparatus similar to a jolly jumper very young children are placed in. This allowed me to put some weight on my legs and feet while keeping me safely suspended. It was not very comfortable, but I was willing to put up with it if it helped me reach my goal. I was also asked to stand, usually holding onto a table. Standing up from my wheelchair still required a great deal of effort and I could not stand unassisted for longer than a minute or so.

Alongside a physical therapist, I had an Occupational Therapist (OT), Blair. Usually, Blair had an assistant. The assistant sat behind me. Her prime objective was to provide support for me. Sometimes the assistant was Lundie. In conversation with her I learned she was on the road to become a physical therapist. I knew she would do well; she had the right mixture of skill and compassion. I would find out many months later that she had indeed written her exam and had become a fully qualified physical therapist.

Blair had me reaching for cones with my right hand. This helped me with balance. By this time, I was able to sit on the edge of the bed for fifteen minutes. Not long perhaps, but much better than the two minutes I was able to do when I left Camrose. Then I would lean back against the therapy assistant and rest. This was about four months post stroke. Looking back, it seems like very slow progress, but when I was there, I was only focused on what I was able to accomplish. Going home was a far-off goal and I was going to walk. I knew the therapy I was getting every day would help me achieve my goal, so I did not pressure anyone to allow me to go home.

Another swallow test was done. I passed. My spirits soared. I was now able to eat regular food with only a few restrictions. I did not have the ability yet to eat and swallow a mixed consistency food such as watery soup or dry cereal with milk. That did not matter! I was eating real food. My first taste of proper food was a piece of toast. I savored the feeling of biting it, chewing it, and then swallowing. It may have been just a piece of bread, but it took me back to the first time I had cotton candy when I was a child. I closed my eyes to savor the moment. The nurse (one of my special angels) who was with me smiled at my wonderment. She was just as pleased with my success as I was! I still had the tube feed because the dietician wanted to make sure that I had enough nourishment. She was afraid I would not be able to eat and swallow enough for my body's needs so I accepted her recommendation. I knew it was only a matter of time before the tube feed was a thing of the past.

About mid-July I asked that my catheter be removed. I had one ever since the stroke. After a stroke, it is common practise to perform an ultrasound after a patient urinates to determine if the patient is retaining urine. If this occurs, a person is more prone to urinary tract infections. Once again, I had to stand up for what I believed was right for me. I was slightly over what was determined the limit of retained urine. I refused an "in and out" procedure. This involves a temporary catheter inserted to totally empty the bladder. I was not going to let them insert one of those again! The nurse accepted my decision graciously. The next trip to the bathroom proved it had been the right one. I gleefully said good-bye permanently to catheters!

Another major event happened. When I went to the physical therapy department and was attempting to do what was asked, Carrie noticed a stain on my shirt. Upon investigation, we discovered my feeding tube had come out. I was ecstatic. As far as I was concerned, I was done with it forever. The doctor insisted on keeping a smaller tube in the opening just in case I needed it. It was easier to go along with the doctor and let time prove me right. This was exactly what happened, mid-July brought a huge shift. I was eating only solid foods, in other words, a regular diet. I felt I was making progress.

What helped me eat regular foods was the help of a fantastic speech therapist. Jocelyn came in the afternoon five days a week. We started with me trying to chew and swallow ice chips. First, I was able to chew and swallow four ice chips out of twenty without coughing. In a few weeks I progressed to eighteen out of twenty without coughing or sputtering. Chewing ice chips and swallowing may not sound like much for therapy but it had great results. Swallowing ice chips helped exercise my throat muscles. Everyone knows that exercise helps build up muscle. If a tiny bit of water got into my lungs from the ice chips my body would simply absorb it with no severe consequences since our body is seventy-five percent water.

I loved the time I spent with her; she was always very supportive. My voice improved but only slightly. It still was barely above a whisper. I do not know why the improvement was minimal. I simply remained grateful that I did have some vocal communication.

Jocelyn had a student who also worked with me. She used an Iowa Oral Performance Instrument (IOPI). This instrument measured tongue strength. I also used it to strengthen my tongue by pressing on a little bulb, first at the front of my mouth then at the back. Unfortunately, her placement ended after about four weeks. About the same time Jocelyn took a position in another hospital. By the end of July, both my therapist and her student had moved on. I was so fortunate to have their help for as long as I did. I was not assigned another speech therapist, I don't know why. Perhaps the people who made the decisions felt my voice was not capable of improving or perhaps the department was only concerned with my swallowing ability. For the remainder of my stay in Red Deer I was given a microphone to amplify my voice. I used it for zoom meetings where it worked beautifully.

I questioned Carrie about my diet. I was losing weight and wanted it to continue. She was adamant that I needed carbohydrates as well as protein. She likened me to a person training for a marathon. I needed the carbs as well as the protein for my body to heal. The brain requires a great deal of calories. In fact, it requires more energy when healing than when just operating normally. Neurons in the brain must grow new pathways for messages to travel on. The procedure is much more complex than a physical injury healing on another part of the body.

    Time passed. Since Alvin was nearly two and a half hours away, he would only come once a week. Lee came with him. Every Sunday they came and visited. When I asked Steve, the department head, if they could both come in, he personally came and measured out the space. Then, when he realized the distance they were travelling, he assured me one way or another it could be made to work. Luckily, we did not need to be creative, the room was just big enough to hold all of us and still maintain a social distance. It did seem silly that they had to sit six feet apart when they rode side by side in the same car, but rules are rules, and I was not going to take a chance and have them told not to come. Although truly, I do not believe that would have happened. Steve would have come up with a solution. He was kind and caring and set a great example to all who worked there.

    Lee continued to come with Alvin until the middle of August when he started working six days a week. The two hours they visited were awesome. The days were sunny and warm, so Lee pushed my chair outside. I was grateful for the chance to escape outdoors.

    So that was my routine the entire summer. Physical therapy twice a day, five days a week, a therapy assistant on Saturdays and Alvin and Lee on Sundays.

    Slowly the constant therapy and hard work was paying off. I was definitely getting stronger. I progressed to using a walker with the help of my physical therapist and an assistant who moved my left foot forward. It was a giant step forward for me. It was the proof I needed to show myself that I would be able to walk eventually. There were still peaks and valleys. I was exhilarated with each tiny bit of improvement. However, I still needed Carrie to remind me of the up and down cycle on days I did not do as well.

Blair, my OT, did not let me slack off either. Every day was an opportunity to work on bathroom activities. First, this consisted of me standing and holding onto a bar. Later, with help, I would use the walker to go to the bathroom. Although I mastered going from my bed to the toilet with an assistant, it would be many months after I got home that I was able to do this on my own. This was partly due to the further distance involved at home and partly because I had to be able to move my left foot myself.

I made a few friends with different patients. One of course, was Penthouse Paul. Two other ladies stick out in my mind. One was the lady from Ponoka who told me I would walk again. If she could come back and use a walker when her doctor told her she would be permanently incapacitated, then I could defy the odds too. She was convinced I would make it happen.

Another lady I also had been with in Ponoka, as well. She was also in her eighties like my first friend. She was recovering from cancer as well as getting therapy because she had her left leg amputated. These two ladies had a great attitude. The second lady was looking forward to driving again. She assured me I would too. Although I did not openly disagree, at that time privately I did not see how this would happen. After all, I couldn't even walk, how was I going to be able to drive. It would not be until I was home for five months, a year after the stroke, that I would even consider this possibility.

Our dining room was becoming full. My friends went home. Others came in their place. Looking at all the others I realized how lucky I was. There were many amputees as well as stroke patients.

One fellow was a double amputee. About twenty years previously, he had one leg amputated. Now he had the second leg done. Thankfully they were both severed below the knee. What amazed me was his attitude. He always appeared pleasant and cheerful and never complained. To me he was an inspiration. If he could get by with two prostheses, then I would learn to walk! After all, I still had both legs, they just needed to learn to work properly!

Many of the other patients were affected by stroke or had brain injuries. There was a young man possibly in his early thirties. His symptoms were very similar to mine. The major difference was his rate of improvement. I had my feeding tube for over four months. His feeding tube was removed within two. I hoped his rate of progress would extend to other areas as well, such as walking etc. His wife and very young son who was less than a year old needed him.

Another patient sticks out in my mind. An older fellow, possibly in his eighties, obviously had a stroke. He had no problem walking or speaking clearly but he had a problem articulating exactly what he wanted to say. At meals he would be upset, but his words did not make sense. Unfortunately, even the nursing staff could not understand what he wanted. Another patient motioned to me that the man was crazy. I was livid. This poor man was desperately trying to communicate, and this lady was making fun of him. What rather amazed me was the depth of the rage I felt. A benefit was that I found my voice. I did not want this lady making fun of him. The word "no" came out easily, clearly, and loudly. Once again, I had hope I would speak normally again.

It bothered me that someone would ridicule a person who had a stroke. I pondered after the event. What was it about this gentleman that scared the lady so much that she had to put him down to make herself feel better? What was there within me that was afraid? Was I concerned that people might look at me and think I was crazy or had a diminished mental capacity? Many people still had a difficult time hearing or completely understanding me.

I know that injustice of any type bothers me. Hence my rage. I had felt the same anger and helplessness when my friend Karen had a stroke several years previously and she seemed to have no one standing up for her. When I visited her almost a year before I had my stroke, she was unable to talk. The only movement she was capable of, was limited to her right hand which allowed her to eat unassisted. By talking to her and maintaining eye contact it was evident she was totally aware and understood what I was saying. At that time, I asked nursing staff about aids that might help her communicate. I was told they could not discuss these types of issues with me since I was only a friend, I was not listed as a contact person. It haunts me that she had no opportunity to have a chance at some rehabilitation. Perhaps I was afraid that I would have no one to stand up for me if I was in a similar situation?

So, what is my lesson in all this? Do I need to stand back and allow others to go about their life without my interference? Even if I can see some small changes that might help, am I to sit helplessly by and do nothing? I pondered over all these questions at length when I was unable to sleep. I was unable to come up with any satisfactory answers.

The middle of August brought another change. Lee was now unable to come with Alvin because of work. He was working twelve-hour shifts, six days a week. I felt he needed his one day off to rest. Fortunately, my friend who was Alvin's niece, Sharon, lived in Red Deer. Since I was only allowed two visitors because of Covid 19, I changed my second person to Sharon. She was awesome. She was there nearly every day. What really made her visits special was the food she brought. I looked forward to her company. She is truly a kind, loving, generous individual whom I love dearly.

About the end of August, the menu changed. The same options appeared week after week. I had a few favorites, and they were no longer offered. Yes, I was definitely improving. I understood what the lady so many months before had said. She was right. The carrots were terrible.

Another huge improvement took place. Transferring by means of a sling became a thing of the past. I progressed to using a slider to transfer from bed to the wheelchair and vice versa. A slider was a slippery, curved board that enabled me to transfer without putting much weight on my feet. In the beginning I needed help to slide along the board. Gradually I became strong enough to move myself onto the board. I only used this for a few weeks before I advanced to a two-person pivot. This was scarier. I would stand, then with help move my right foot which was more mobile. The second person would move my left foot. Then I could turn and sit on the chair or the bed. Thankfully within a very short time I progressed to a one-person transfer. Again, scary at first, but as I gained strength, it became a bit easier. I was improving and I could see a glimmer of light at the end of the tunnel. My goal of going home was becoming a reality.

Also, if I was going to go home, I had to remind my body to use the bathroom. It was probably comparable to new parents toilet training their little ones. However, in my case, I was in control and watched the time and decided when to use the toilet. The use of running water helped. Ask anyone who needs to pee and hears water running. I didn't get much warning when I had to eliminate solids, but thankfully nursing staff were quick to answer since I did not use my call bell often.

My final review was in September. I was to stay in Red Deer for one more month. This was probably one month more than most patients stayed. The final month was more of the same, day after day with therapy. Carrie also had me sidestepping at the bars. Three steps one way and then three steps back, had me looking longingly at my chair. Gratefully I would grab onto it and sit down. Since there was a three step "staircase", I mentioned to Carrie I would like to try stairs. Her reply was "not yet." I can now understand why. It was many months after I returned home that I was ready for that step.

Another step forward for me was walking along a hall banister holding on with my right hand. Only using my right hand for support gave me the illusion of walking unaided. With a helper moving my left foot I was able to walk at least twenty feet. This gave me renewed confidence and determination. I would walk again unaided.

I was also fitted with an ankle foot orthotic (AFO). An AFO will keep the foot from dropping so walking is easier. I used the AFO for four to five months after I got home, at which time I was given a much smaller one which fit into my regular running shoe.

The end of September brought my discharge date which I eagerly awaited. I was to make a stop and stay at the Tofield Hospital until my home was inspected and found satisfactory to meet my needs.

Then the big day arrived. The ambulance personnel transferred me to their stretcher. As I was wheeled out, one EMT was amazed at the tears in the eyes of many of the staff. "I have never seen this before", she said. I was a bit overwhelmed myself. I loved all of them and I knew the entire staff was wishing me well. They all hold a special place in my heart; the staff who came with me from Ponoka, the new staff who also showed me great care and compassion, and the entire therapy departments. I believe it was because of the therapists and assistants that I have progressed as much as I have. Yes, I worked hard but what made it easier was the constant support and encouragement. I remember Carrie telling me "You can say, I told you so" when referring to my walking. I could not do that yet. In my eyes, I was still not properly walking.

There was communication between the Red Deer and Tofield therapy departments to ensure a smooth transition. Red Deer did everything they could to ensure I would get some therapy to keep improving. Unfortunately, Tofield did not follow through immediately. I am guessing this was due to the lack of communication. The OT department, which was contacted, only works part-time.

"Gratitude unlocks the fullness of life."
Melody Beattie

Chapter 7
Tofield

I met my new doctor in Tofield upon my arrival. She appeared to listen, so I was totally prepared to have her as my doctor. I arrived on Tuesday and told her I would be going home by Friday. Because renovations were not complete, I would go home on a pass Friday and return Monday for two more days.

The renovations were quite extensive. First of all, a ramp needed to be constructed so I could enter with my wheelchair. Many years previously at Christmas when my mother who was wheelchair bound visited, my husband physically pulled the chair up the step into the house and then around a corner and up another step. To do this on a regular basis would be exhausting for my husband who is seventy years of age.

Also on the renovation agenda was the bathroom. I was not able to get into the bathtub or out of it. The tub was removed, a window above where the tub had been was covered up, and a wheelchair accessible shower was installed. The total cost of the renovations exceeded twenty-one thousand dollars. Thankfully there was a provincial grant which did cover one third of the cost. I shudder at the burden that less fortunate people carry if they do not have any savings.

I was surprised when I did not get a visit from any therapists. I knew Red Deer had contacted Tofield. I also knew I would not get the intense therapy which I had in

Red Deer but surely, I would receive some. A therapist came and assisted my roommate who had a wrenched shoulder. "He would come to me later in the day," he assured me. Friday came and I still had not seen a therapist. My days were spent in bed or on a chair. It was hard not to be disappointed. I could understand this was just a regular hospital but surely even fifteen minutes every other day could be arranged.

The weekend home gave me a respite from hospital life. Being together with Alvin for an entire two days was heavenly. He did an excellent job of looking after me but unfortunately Sunday evening arrived and it was time to go back to the hospital. The next two days followed the same pattern as the previous week. Nursing staff helped me to the bathroom and then back to a chair. There was absolutely no hint of any assistance to help me help myself.

Tuesday arrived and I escaped the confines of the hospital to my beloved home. I was both relieved and elated at the same time. I was relieved because I was definitely not going into any type of facility. Any remaining vestiges of the specture of going into a nursing home were banished. I was elated because I was finally home. Coming into our driveway I felt the sense of peace that envelopes me whenever I gaze upon our yard. The many trees shield us from the outside world. Our yard is our own little piece of heaven on earth.

The next day my husband attempted to assist me in walking but one week of no physical activity had made an impact on my body. My knees gave way and he helped me gently to the floor. Both of us were extremely concerned.

The next day I was visited at home by a number of people which included the OT from Tofield. We made it very clear I needed help which not only included home care but extra therapy. I had already regressed and neither one of us was very happy.

Thankfully the OT arranged for me to be accepted in the Early Stroke Discharge (ESD) Program from Camrose for a period of eight weeks. I was overjoyed. Showing gratitude had paid off once again. In the beginning of the program, I had about two home visits and three via zoom per week. By the end, Covid was once again prevalent, and I only had one home visit and all the others via zoom. I made huge progress in those eight weeks. I started using my cane more than my walker and with the help of my physical therapist, I navigated the one big step and one small one between our main house and our addition. Wow! Again, I give a lot of credit to all the therapists and their assistants. It was because of their assistance and encouragement that I was able to do as well as I did. One assistant even demonstrated how to vacuum while I was sitting in the wheelchair. What a boost to my mental health. The therapy assistant showed me I was not useless around the house.

One session something totally unexpected happened. A therapist came with a beautiful winter coat with a fur trimmed hood. It was short in the back which meant less bulk in the wheelchair. The sleeves were formed by snaps so there was no struggle putting it on. The front was extra long so it covered the wearer's legs when sitting in the wheelchair. She asked me if I wanted it. I was very touched and accepted it thankfully. Even now, a year later my heart warms when I put on the coat and I say a brief prayer of gratitude for this person's gracious gift.

The speech pathologist with the program referred me to an Ear, Nose, and Throat (ENT) Specialist to rule out any physical problems with my larynx or throat which might be affecting my voice quality.

During all this time my husband helped me walk five or six days a week. At first it was one trip across the kitchen with a rest every time. Eventually it was a trip across the kitchen and back and then a rest. All things inevitably come to an end. The middle of December came, and I finished the Early Stroke Discharge Program.

In Alberta, there is a program called Home Care designed to help keep seniors and other disabled people in their homes instead of in a facility. I was approved for this program, so I had Home Care twice a day. Mornings they helped me wash and get dressed for the day. Evenings they assisted me in getting ready for bed. As well, every Thursday I would get a shower and they would stay for another two hours to allow Alvin time to run into Edmonton and pick up whatever we needed, such as groceries, medication, or anything else on our list. Thursday was also sheet changing day. With home care doing ninety to ninety-five percent of the work and myself doing the remainder, it was a job that my husband gladly abdicated his responsibility from. It was also on Thursdays that I, with the help of Home Care, vacuumed or cleaned cupboards.

Apparently one aide complained about cleaning in the pantry. This was not written up in their list of duties. When I was questioned about it, I said I was not going to have them sit there and watch me. I did not need a babysitter. The following Thursday I was planning on reorganizing my linen shelf and I would require assistance with this since it was difficult for me to take out dish towels etc. and put them on the table. So, to prevent further complaints (which it did) job descriptions were changed so they could help me with various tasks. A stipulation was made that they would assist me while I was doing something. I did not mind since I was already doing this. Since the change to their job description was made, there have been no complaints.

It may sound as if I am being picky; I don't believe I am. However, I have learned to stand up and advocate for myself to people in authority; because I was truly grateful for the service they provided, the Home Care girls in turn treated me with care and compassion.

What shocked me was that a Home Care Coordinator told me she was surprised I had come home since I required so much care. I was livid! Did she really expect me to be in an institution? After I calmed down, I realized she meant that my husband really had to assist me a lot. And, it was true, if it were not for him life would have been much more difficult. However, I would not have progressed to this extent in an institution. I am not impressed with the level of care residents receive in long term care facilities.

Since I was not getting any more therapy, I asked if Home Care could assist me with exercises. I was told no. I already had maxed out on the time I was allotted. I found this interesting since it was a home care aide who had suggested the idea to me. Apparently, they did help other patients with walking etc.

About this same time, I participated in a program called GRASP which is sponsored by the March of Dimes. For one hour every week we were led through hand exercises and then were expected to do them an hour every day. I had a hard time doing this every day, but I did make some progress. Perhaps it was not as much as I had hoped for, but I celebrated each tiny step forward. It was my left hand that was the primary focus. When the program started, I could only stack blocks with the left hand being assisted by the right. By the end of the program, I was able to do it using the left only. I could not stack them very high, only three or four blocks, but it was an improvement nonetheless.

Perhaps the most disheartening fact about this program was that I had already completed many similar tasks with my right hand three or four months earlier. However, instead of dwelling on the seemingly repetitive nature of my therapy, I chose to be happy that my more severely affected side was responding.

"Your life is the manifestation of your dream; it is an art. You can change your life anytime you are not enjoying the dream."
Don Miguel Ruiz

Chapter 8.
More Hard Work

A new year came upon us. January, 2021 rolled around. Covid was still maintaining its heavy grasp upon us. It did not affect me too much since getting about in a wheelchair is difficult with snow covered sidewalks. Staying home was an easy choice. However, I really missed seeing my family and I was limited to the number of visitors that were allowed.

A fact that I had never noticed or considered before my stroke was how difficult it is to get around in a wheelchair onto sidewalks off the street even in the handicapped areas. The snow is rarely scraped off completely and pushing the wheelchair is a difficult task for the caregiver.

My appointment with the ENT revealed there were no apparent physical blockages to my speech. I was so fortunate that the Early Stroke Discharge (ESD) group in Camrose had referred me to another speech pathologist. It was back to practising long e's and ah's. The word bumblebee was added to my repertoire. Below is a graph that illustrates my progression. Although this particular graph was for speech exercises, the entire rehab process followed this pattern.

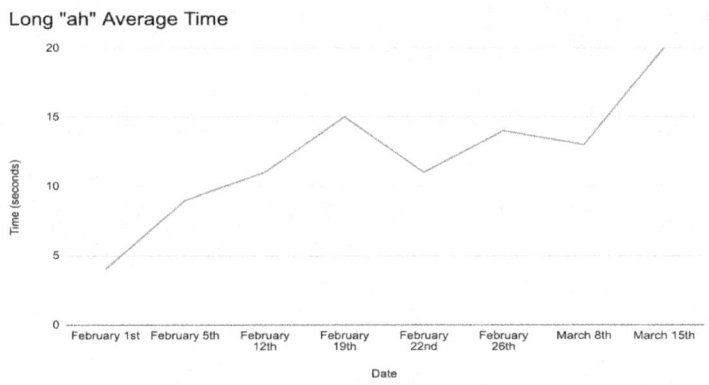

  Then something wonderful happened. Tofield hired a new physiotherapist. I was impressed with Dan, this young Australian chap. I would equate him with Carrie, my therapist from Red Deer both in knowledge and caring. At the same time, I had a therapy assistant, Sandra Dee, come out with him to see what therapy was suggested. Dan also felt I needed more help than I was presently receiving in order to progress further. I explained I was already getting all the time I was allowed with Home Care.

  When Dan asked what my goals were, I mentioned climbing the six steps in my son's house. This time there was no hint that this goal was not attainable. The assistant was given instructions on how this might be achieved. Unfortunately, this young man did not stay long. He received a better offer elsewhere and left. I am not sure what he wrote in his notes but I received a phone call from a home care nurse asking how much time would be needed for my exercises. I could not believe my good fortune. Not wanting to be overly greedy, I suggested fifteen minutes. First, bed exercises were tried. Then there were complaints about the possibilities of back injuries and the exercises were halted. I was deeply disappointed. My disappointment did not last long. Possibly two weeks later I was informed they would start again but using only sit-to-stand. This consisted of me in the wheelchair, sitting with the left foot slightly behind the right, standing up, putting all of my weight on my left foot, standing on it for ten seconds, then sitting down. I was to do three sets of ten. In the beginning I would do five, rest, then finish the ten. Of course, I had to do this three times. Eventually, I would complete a set of ten and then rest. Small improvements but at least there was progress.

Another new physical therapist, Nicole joined the Tofield department. When she came out with the Sandra Dee, they would have me side-stepping up the ramp while holding onto the railing. The first time I made three passes. The second time, a week later, I made four. All this hard work was preparation for me to climb the stairs at my son's house. Thankfully Nicole approved of the regimen Dan had suggested. The sit-to-stands were good strengthening exercises. When I was able to do ten of these easily, she suggested doing twelve. At the same time, I would bear weight on my left foot and let my right foot merely help me balance. The next progression was to place one foot on a step and maintain balance for ten seconds. This presented much more of a challenge. Many weeks would pass before this became easier. Home Care aides would stand beside me and keep track of time so I would meet the criteria that was set for me.

I only knew one lady when Home Care first started coming. Now I have many new friends who only want me to keep improving and are my main cheerleaders whenever I make progress.

In about February, not quite a year after my stroke, I was able to hold a key down on my laptop with my left hand. I loved playing solitaire on my laptop and this was now much easier.

Five months after my stroke, while I was still in Red Deer, one of my friends told me I would drive again. I didn't believe it was possible. Eleven months after the stroke I decided to renew my driver's license with the intention of perhaps driving the few kilometers into Ryley. So, in June, fifteen months after my stroke, I went into the registration office and renewed my license. As I get stronger, I set new goals.

A good example of new goals is my wheelchair. In December, the OT made an appointment for me to attend a seating clinic. A seating clinic determines the best seat and backing a wheelchair should have. She suggested a one arm drive since my left arm still was not very functional. When I got my trial chair in January, I loved it; I was able to get about the house much easier. I did have a niggling doubt. I wanted to use my left hand too, to strengthen it. In May, I had another seating clinic and another trial chair. If I was to order a wheelchair in May, it would be a regular two hand drive. Since changing my mind at this point in time would probably add additional time to getting it, I just decided to go with the one arm drive chair that was previously ordered.

I am finding I am needing to be the judge of what I can or cannot do. In the early days of the stroke, I was exceptionally tired. What I learned is this was simply due to the fact I had a major stroke. Since the body was healing and the rehabilitation process takes up a lot of energy, it is very common to feel tired. Even one year later my body needs to rest often, especially when attempting new tasks. The major difference is that I am able to accomplish more and need a bit less time to recuperate. As time progresses, I feel my body getting stronger.

At the end of April, we had our rugs replaced with vinyl so I would have access to the entire main floor. Since our house was not made to accommodate wheelchairs the doors and door frames to the bathroom were becoming horribly scuffed. Our carpenter retouched the paint when he refinished our floors. Because I did not want the scuffs to reappear, I had incentive to walk into the bathroom instead of having home care push me in.

Alvin was usually the only person I allowed to wheel me in. I could trust him to avoid the door frames.

One major effect of stroke that many people do not know about, or mention is heightened emotions. I found myself emotional about anything. One time in a discussion about Ukraine and its history with being downtrodden and conquered I could barely speak because of the tears. I spoke with an aide and she related similar struggles that one of her family members had. Apparently, this man had several similar experiences. In addition, he had been working at a job he loved, then due to the stroke was no longer able to communicate as effectively and as a consequence was no longer able to do his job as a teacher. Coupled with the fact that he was a man and six feet tall, our society in general does not accept weepy men. I decided then that I would simply stop judging myself and accept the person I now was.

"It does not matter how slowly you go so long as you do not stop."
Confucius

Chapter 9
Keep Going

Throughout my whole journey I have been grateful for all the help I have received. There have been times when I almost gave in and wallowed in self-pity. It is disheartening to not be able to change positions in bed or dress myself. Through perseverance I was finally able to turn onto my left side in bed. This was about fourteen months after my stroke. It may be difficult to turn but it is possible. If I have any advice to offer anyone it is this, "Don't give up!"

Some people find it beneficial to write down their goals. I even did a vision board a few years before I had the stroke. One of my goals had been to have my house remodelled. This happened but not until after my stroke. It seems that even though I am the key player in my game of life, I am also on the sidelines watching. I didn't have to reset a goal of getting my house redone; I knew it was happening.

I have had one major goal in mind, to walk. I have not had to visualize it, to imagine it. I just kept working on it, knowing it would happen. Most people would say "I'll believe it when I see it; for myself it's believing it, knowing it in every fibre of my body and then it will happen. This is due in large part to influences of reading books by Wayne Dyer, Eckhart Tolle and many others. I choose to believe that I will continue to improve. In conversation with a family member, she said hope is essential for success. For myself, hope is not the requirement, knowing is. To me, hope means you have a possibility. Knowing something makes it happen. I have never hoped I would walk again; I have known it will happen. And slowly but surely with perseverance and hard work it is happening.

A little success came about the end of April. I was able to pull and tear toilet paper off the roll. I finally had enough strength in my right hand to give a hard enough yank to tear it off. When I am disappointed in my slow progress I think back to that tiny victory. I suggest you try tearing off toilet paper with one hand. It is not as easy as you might believe, or perhaps, I was not as strong as I thought I was.

Another huge turning point was teaching a first aid class for my granddaughter. I spent the entire day talking with a few breaks here and there. This was a major accomplishment for someone who at one point was incapable of making a sound. All this was the result of practising the e's and ah's as well as the word bumblebee. The class took place at the end of April. Another class for the other granddaughters took place at the end of May. This time there were four people instead of one. The classes were not done the way I taught previously, I did not demonstrate the way I did pre-stroke, but I am confident these young people have a basic knowledge of first aid and Cardio Pulmonary Resuscitation (CPR). I know I did a good job!

With May and June came warmer weather which means I had the opportunity to plant and care for peas and cucumbers in what were previously my flower pots. I am very capable and glad to be able to accomplish these small tasks.

I continue to attend speech therapy twice a week. One day is for practising my vowels and the second is a conversation group. Both sessions are via zoom. It was here that I met two very interesting individuals. One is quite young; when you are nearing seventy anyone in their thirties is young. I had not realized that people in their twenties and thirties could have strokes. I knew that fevers with very high temperatures could induce seizures but that was not the case here. Thankfully the drug TPA was administered and the resulting disability was not as severe as it could have been.

Another lady had a very interesting perspective. "Everything will be okay in the end," she said. "If it's not okay, it's not the end." That phrase has stuck with me.

This whole experience with the stroke has reiterated what I believe. Keep your faith and trust that all is in divine order. You are never given more than you can handle. An attitude of gratitude will move you through anything.

A friend once told me "You should give with the expectation of being rewarded in some way." I prefer to give with no expectation and allow the universe to work its magic.

Never once did I think or say "Why did this happen to me? Why did God allow this to happen?" For one thing, I do not believe in a vengeful God. Making these types of statements is a sign of spiritual immaturity and drags us into victimhood. We can choose to sit in judgement of ourselves and others or we can take the gift we are given and look within. Again, I repeat, we are not given more than we can handle.

Along the way we will meet many teachers. Some will be warm, compassionate, and caring. Others will make us angry. These perhaps are the ones we really need to pay attention to. What is it within us that we may be afraid of, that we do not accept?

Fifteen months after the stroke I can finally stand at the sink alone, with my cane by my side and brush my teeth and wash my hands.

A major achievement came about mid-June. My son Lee was fixing his house to put it on the market. My husband went over and offered his help. I tagged along. Both of them pulled my chair up the big step outside the house. Inside was the challenge. The house is a bi-level. There were six steps to the main floor. With Lee beside me holding me, and Alvin behind me moving and lifting my feet I made it to the top of the stairs. The first two steps I was able to lift my right foot myself, the others required more assistance. The recliner was a welcome haven. When we left for the evening on Saturday it was a hilarious process. I sat on the top step, my husband pulled my feet while my son lifted under my arms so I would gently slide down to the next step. We repeated the process of going up the stairs on the following day, Sunday. However when we were going home, I insisted on walking down, with help of course. I felt this was much more dignified.

Fifteen months after the stroke I was able to sit up and get out of bed and into my wheelchair. Quite an accomplishment for someone who could only manage to sit for two minutes on the side of the bed one year previously! I continue to keep getting out of bed by myself. It gives me a bit of independence and allows my husband more freedom to do his work.

"If you can't fly, then run
If you can't run, then walk
If you can't walk, then crawl
But whatever you do, you have to keep moving forward."
Martin Luther King, Jr.

Chapter 10
And Still Keeping Going

About this time, I had an episode of depression. It was not serious, and I did not require medication, but my heart felt heavy nonetheless. It had been fifteen months since my stroke, and I still needed help showering and dressing as well as getting into bed. In addition, getting into a vehicle took a lot of effort and help. I was a bit more independent, but I was far from being able to be alone for twenty-four hours. In addition, pre-stroke I jumped in the car and went wherever I wanted, whenever I wanted. I still had such a long way to go and I was tired of the constant exercises.

Thankfully, I confided in a health care aide with whom I had become good friends. She gave me some good advice which is appropriate for anyone who has gone through a similar health challenge. It was simply this. "Allow yourself to feel what you are feeling. Don't stuff it down. Cry if you need to. Yell if you need to. You have a right to your feelings. You have been through a lot".

I also remembered a friend from Red Deer. Remembering her advice made me smile. "If you are feeling sad, cry your heart out. Cry for twenty minutes. Don't hold anything back. Then you can stop crying and think about something else."

My dear friend and speech therapist Kelsey also gave me some insight. Although the following is not a word for word transcript, I feel I have captured the essence of what she said.

"If you think about the last year and a half there have been some major losses. You are grieving for what you have lost. Sometimes there isn't a way to fix the feelings, no way to just move on from them. You just need to allow yourself to feel your feelings. If you skip out of the garbage feelings, you miss out on the good feelings too. Apparently, this is just part of being human. Allowing yourself to feel those feelings does not mean you are bad or you are weak. It doesn't mean you are not trying. This does not mean it is a bad recovery."

I mentioned that I was also tired of doing the physical therapy. I was wondering if I was just getting lazy, I didn't want to do the prescribed therapy the physical therapist told me to, day after day.

Her response was that people were not inherently lazy. "If you do not do something, it is because there is a blockage, something is holding you back." She also reminded me of the peaks and valleys on the road to recovery. "The road forward is not a straight line uphill."

This was what I needed to hear at that point in time. I do not suggest that anyone who is going through depression does not need more help. Counselling or even medication might be appropriate so please seek help if you feel yourself stuck in that state for a long period of time. However, I am just sharing with you what worked for me. For the most part I was and still am a positive person. I do my best to maintain a positive attitude and look with gratitude upon all that happens in my life. But I have also decided that sometimes a good cry can also help me feel better.

*"No one saves us but ourselves. No one can and no one may.
We ourselves must walk the path."*
Buddha

Chapter 11
Little Victories

With a new month, July, came the lifting of restrictions in the province of Alberta. Gatherings were now allowed without masks and there were no limits on the number of people in one place. I attended a Combine Crunch put on by the Hardisty Rodeo Association. A combine crunch is merely a handful of individuals driving old combines which are no longer used for harvesting who try to demolish their opponents by smashing into them. A combine crunch is comparable to a demolition derby where vehicles are used for this purpose.

It was held after the rodeo and chuckwagon races. The stands were full. What I totally enjoyed was people coming and speaking with me. Usually I am the social butterfly, going out and about, meeting and interacting with others. Our son, who was part of the Association, also won first place. His combine was the last machine running. It felt so good to be able to come, support him, and applaud him.

I keep mentioning gratitude. How can a person in this situation be grateful? Well, our son arranged for us to park our vehicle beside the grandstand so we could have an unobstructed view. Both my husband and I appreciated this concern and front row seating.

July seemed to be all about firsts. About the time I was wondering if I was ever going to improve, my husband

and I paid Lee another visit. Sixteen months after my stroke on July 23, 2021, with only the help of Lee, I climbed all six steps to the main floor of his bi-level. Going down when we were leaving was much trickier. I needed the assistance of both Alvin and Lee. We repeated the same process the next day. Again, I required only one assistant going up and two assistants coming down. I think I needed reassurance that the first day had not been a fluke, a chance occurrence.

The second accomplishment or as I put it, the icing on the cake, so to speak, came a day later. I drove my Durango to a neighbors' place where my husband was going to bale hay. With Alvin on the tractor in front and myself following pulling a piece of equipment called a hayrake, we drove approximately four miles. Not far perhaps, and Alvin had to help me in and out of the vehicle, but it was a step forward. It may be some time before I am able to venture on my own but at least now I can see the possibility of that happening.

The next small victory or third success was baking a saskatoon pie by myself. I asked Alvin to put all the ingredients on the cupboard and I cheated by using an already made store bought crust, but I mixed it all up and managed to put it into the oven myself. This was a bit difficult since my left hand doesn't cooperate but I did do it myself. However, when it was baked, I asked Home Care to take it out. I was not going to take a chance on dropping it! It looked and smelled good, and I was not going to let the hard work go to waste!

I am now getting stronger and can help Alvin by washing the kitchen sink and cleaning the cupboard counters. Yes, it takes me twice as long as an able-bodied person, but it does give me a sense of purpose and helps my husband who is still busy with welding jobs, haying and all the yard work that I did at one time. What I found frustrating is that I was unable to stand for longer than a couple of minutes. I would have to sit and rest then I could stand again. My sense of balance also needs to improve. I believe it will.

My plans for my next respite day (the day home care stays for an extra two hours) involved making muffins. Alvin brought all the ingredients to the kitchen counter and I with the help of my aide measured, mixed, and filled the muffin tins. Then, while they were in the oven, I washed the dishes we used, and my aide dried them. My only regret was she had to leave before they were baked, and I could not give her a sample. Since I was having a craving for brownies, they would probably be on the agenda very soon.

My last first for the month was astounding to me. I give a lot of credit for this accomplishment to both Nicole and Sandra Dee. I managed to get into bed myself. When I had tried it a month previously, it was impossible. My therapists suggested a wooden block to stand on. Still, no success. I simply could not get enough momentum to lift my left leg high enough. It seemed an insurmountable task. This time a different tactic was used. By changing the head of the bed to the opposite end, I swung my right leg up first. With my right foot on the bed, I had enough strength to drag and lift my left. My therapists and I decided to try the opposite side of the bed since the headboard would be in the right place. It worked very well. I was exhausted from doing this four times in a row, but I was also exhilarated. I was doing it! I was getting into bed by myself! There were a couple of glitches. That side of the bed was very close to the wall. The wheelchair and commode I used at night could not fit in. Because I was groggy and half asleep and I did not trust myself to walk to the bathroom at night, I used the commode. One solution was to move our bed over so there was more room. This way the head of the bed could remain where it was. Because our mattresses were on a waterbed frame, the whole unit would have to be dismantled to move. This process would take several hours. In talking with my husband, we both agreed using the foot of our bed as the new head would be a better solution. Since he is very resourceful, he will come up with a metal headboard that will attach to the foot of the bed. We will probably be the only folks around who have two headboards!

Perhaps most importantly, I have renewed determination that I will be getting in and out of vehicles myself and going into town myself. I seem to be in a pattern of accomplishing something, feeling great about it, then feeling bad when I am unable to accomplish that same task the next day. I need to remember the road to recovery has peaks and valleys; it is not a straight line.

"Our greatest glory is not in never falling but in rising every time we fall."
Confucius

Chapter 12
Light At The End Of The Tunnel

August arrived and our hot weather continued. I was glad to stay indoors where our air conditioner ran continuously. During the cooler evenings I ventured outdoors. Although I love summer, baking in the hot sun is not something I enjoy doing. Being fair-skinned I tend to burn easily and can quickly look like a boiled lobster.

I was able to pick enough raspberries that Alvin and I had a delicious treat. Another accomplishment was picking the Nanking Cherries which Alvin turned into juice. The last bit of cherries we used for making liqueur.

Alvin finished the new headboard and I couldn't wait for the paint to dry so I could try getting into bed by myself.

A trip to Red Deer was undertaken to see my physiatrist, Dr. McLean. As I expected everything was fine. The bonus for me was seeing my physical therapists and occupational therapist and showing off my accomplishments. One of my nursing "angels" came to the hospital to see me as well. My heart sang.

Another plus for me was visiting Sharon and her husband. We stayed for a delicious supper, then a trip up three stairs to the washroom which I needed a lot of help with, and we were on our way home. I could have been disappointed with the amount of help I needed but I chose to reflect on the long day I had and decided it was a normal consequence.

Another small victory was getting dressed by myself. Although not something I did every day, I proved to myself it was not impossible. Dressing takes much, much longer so it is reserved for weekend mornings when Home Care does not come so I am not using up valuable exercise time. "You are using all the allocated time" still is vivid in my memory and I do not wish to jeopardize the amount of time home care aides are allowed to spend with me. However, what this does, is it shows me there will indeed come a time when I may no longer need their assistance.

As expected, there are days I get in and out of bed by myself. Then, there are days these tasks seem impossible, and I require assistance. I simply remind myself the road to recovery is not a straight line.

One day I spent an entire hour vacuuming our SUV. Because we live in the country and we travel on gravel roads much of the time, and also because it has become our main mode of transportation since it is easier for me to exit, it had become quite filthy. Keeping our vehicles clean had been my responsibility and I was quite happy to resume this duty. The next occasion that I go out with my husband I can wipe down the dashboard etc. since I still require assistance getting into the Durango. I was exhausted with the amount of effort I expended; it was comparable to my one-hour therapy sessions with Carrie in Red Deer. However, since Alvin brought the vacuum cleaner outside, I was able to do all the cleaning myself, including adding an extension cord to reach around to the other side of the vehicle. To someone who has two hands which function very well, this is no big deal. For myself, with one good hand and a questionable sense of balance, this work took more effort and concentration.

There is also the glimmer of hope I will within the next year, be able to descend the thirteen steps to the basement. Of course, coming up will require more energy but I am confident I will be able to do it. To me, this will be the ultimate proof that I will have made a near complete recovery. At this point in time, I also hope to be getting in my vehicle myself and exiting safely as well. The possibility of Home Care no longer needing to come twice daily is a strong possibility as well. I am not in a hurry to dispense with their services since I value the time they spend with me doing exercises.

Although this stroke was not something I relished, it certainly gave me lessons in patience with myself, perseverance, and showed me the benefits of hard work. Gratitude to all those around me made difficult days easier to bear.

*"A wise man adapts himself to circumstances,
as water shapes itself to the vessel that contains it."*
Chinese Proverb

Chapter 13
Brett's Story

The cooler temperatures of September were a welcome relief after the hot sweltering summer. The high teens were a welcome change from the 27°C to the low 30°C. Any trip, even if it was just for groceries was met with pleasure. I enjoyed seeing the combines working away in the fields. Harvest was in full swing.

My progress on the other hand was at a much slower pace than I liked. I was continuing my sit-to-stand exercises with Home Care five days a week. In addition, I had a pulley system on my bedroom door. I pulled down with my right hand which raised my left hand. The primary purpose of this system was to keep the left arm limber and also increase its range of motion. I was also exercising my left hand and arm sporadically. Stacking blocks on top of each other and moving the hand back and forth in an arc on the table were on the agenda. I was so tired of doing these, but I knew I would not get better if I did nothing. I did see a small degree of improvement when I was doing arm curls. I would hold the left arm as straight as I could, then bend it at the elbow and bring my hand towards my shoulder. Originally in December of the previous year when I had done the arm curls, I used my phone as a weight. It was approximately six ounces. Now, nine months later I am using a three-pound weight. My right hand still assisted but it was gratifying to see the improvement.

I joined several stroke survivor groups on Facebook. It was good to talk with others who had similar experiences. To some people I would offer encouragement, others were an inspiration. I want to share a story by Brett, a stroke survivor, who graciously gave me his permission to use his story. The story is in his own words.

"Happy celebrate life day everyone! 14yrs ago today I had my stroke. I had a very sharp pain behind my left eye all day, but being 21 years old I figured it couldn't be anything more than a headache. I went over to my friend's house for a game of poker and couldn't shake the pain. I remember looking down at my cards and they were so blurry I couldn't make out my hand. Migraines run in my family, although I never get them, so that explained the headache and blurred vision. No biggie. I looked up from my cards and my blurred friends were moving their lips, but the sound coming out was like the teacher on charlie brown- incoherent noise.

I played a few hands, bluffing and doing my best to alleviate the pressure between my ears. I stood up to go to the bathroom and felt the whole floor shift. In the bathroom the lights were intense and trippy. It honestly felt like the beginning of a mushroom trip. Woozy, confusion, shifting floors, electric beach towels hanging in the bathroom. Cold water on my face was the only thing to bring me back down. I finished the poker game, hugged my friends, and drove home. I say the word "drove" very lightly. I floated home under intense street lights is more fitting.

I stumbled up the stairs when I got home, popped a few ibuprofen, and threw up all night.

I woke in the morning to the doorbell ringing. My roommates had already left for class so I went downstairs to find my girlfriend at the door. We got in a small fight about whether I should go to the hospital or not. I'm a stubborn guy and I still thought it was a migraine. After some back and forth she kissed me and went to class. 15 minutes later my mom showed up. Lindsay had called her and told her all about how sick I was.

We went to the youth clinic, because I was 21 and invincible and hadn't been to the doctor in years. My childhood doctor quickly urged us to go to the ER. It could be anything from a migraine, to west Nile virus, to the aneurysm that I eventually found out I had. At the ER they had a strong suspicion that it was west Nile or encephalitis and I was being prepped for a lumbar puncture. The nurse came in and said that as a precaution I needed a CT scan just in case. That's when they found my aneurysm.

I was rushed down to Denver (about 60miles away) to get brain surgery. I just remember this crazy feeling of losing all control. "It's all out of my hands now, and the only thing I can control is how I respond" I remember saying to myself as I was being rushed in for surgery.

The next thing I remember is being awoken by a doctor. He explained what had just happened and asked me to move my right side. I looked to my right and did everything in my power to flail my arms, wiggle my toes, throw an elbow, lift a leg, but I got nothing. I got cold, wet, sandbags. It was one of those dreams where your legs feel like cement and you can't run. I looked to my left side and everything was moving, trying out of frustration to show my right side how to do it, and a tear rolled down my cheek.

2 weeks in the ICU learning what had just happened and letting my brain heal. The doctors said that it's likely I wouldn't walk again and that I had an 80% chance of mortality upon arrival. I was walking with my walker by the time I left the ICU for inpatient rehab.

Another 2 weeks in inpatient relearning life skills like tying my shoe, feeding myself, and getting dressed. I was walking with a cane by the time I left inpatient for my parent's house.

Months and months of intense outpatient rehab. My girlfriend who saved my life ended up breaking up with me. My emotions had taken control of me and would swing drastically (I blame kepra). Plus, we were young. No one taught us how to deal with an event like that. I channeled everything I had into my rehab. I enrolled back in school at csu and became that 22 year old with a cane stumbling to class. I had to relearn how to use my filter and control my emotions. I can't begin to tell you how important meditation was for that part of my life. I ended up getting asked to teach the class on recovery from brain injury in my neuropsychology class. Things got easier with a lot of hard work. I got to the point in part where I was running, albeit very poorly.

14 years later and I am still working on things. Everyday I deal with my stroke. Some things only I notice. But you have to keep on going. I share my story not to gloat about what I've overcome, but In case some of you need a little kick in the ass. We've had to deal with something that 99% of the world will never understand, so this battle is only with yourself. Some days suck. They beat the shit out of you and you feel worthless. Fight back. Beat life. Prove everyone wrong. It's either that or accept where you are and deal with your situation. Either way, this is our second life. Not too many people get a second life so make

it what you will. Embrace it. Embrace your faults. Walking differently than everyone else is a little funny sometimes. It's a little funny how I get a slur after having a drink or two. This is our life, celebrate it!

Sorry for such a long post btw! Kudos if you read it all Happy Celebrate life day!!!"

When I feel sorry for myself, I read Brett's post. I was sixty-eight when I had my stroke. He was only twenty-one. Imagine your life turned upside down at that age. The point is, he did not give up!

Many of the younger people who have had strokes have had aneurysms. The only consolation, if there is any, to having a stroke at a younger age is that the rate of healing appears to be much quicker.

If you, the reader, have suffered a stroke I strongly suggest checking out Facebook for stroke survivor groups. A caregiver will also benefit from checking out these groups as well. There are many different stories, many different ages at which people have strokes. Belonging to groups such as those may help alleviate feelings of loneliness and isolation. For myself, many of the people are a source of inspiration. I have also learned I am not unique in not having had the classical symptoms. I read of a lady who was having difficulty with her hand. She was astounded to find out she had a stroke because there were no other symptoms. There are also stroke survivors who have gone to the hospital and then were sent home only to return a few hours later with a full-blown stroke. My only advice is if anyone has any symptoms that are possibly stroke related to seek medical attention. With CT scans a quicker and more accurate diagnosis is possible.

> *"We are what we repeatedly do.*
> *Excellence, therefore, is not an act but a habit."*
> *Aristotle*

Chapter 14
Slow Changes

When I came home in October of 2020, I was under the impression I was only allowed only one assisted shower per week with Home Care. For several months Alvin would help me take a second shower. Then he got busy with work and it became too much of a burden. Fast forward one year to October 2021. When one of the Home Care Aides mentioned that a year previously the Government of Alberta had mandated all recipients of Home Care receive two showers, I was disappointed that I had not been told of this development. However, instead of dwelling on the unfairness, I chose to look forward to my second shower. There were a few obstacles to be overcome before this would happen. First, I was told the shower would need to happen at 1 P.M. on Saturday. Since I do not receive Home Care Saturday mornings this would mean I would need to stay in my pyjamas until 1:00p.m. or have my husband dress me in morning, have Home Care come and shower me at 1:00, redress me, then return at 6:00 to help me into my pyjamas. This seemed to be a very inefficient use of Home Care. As well, I would not be able to plan any daylong trips for Saturday. The immediate supervisors agreed to switch the showers to Saturday evening. Then, apparently the immediate supervisors were overruled. Once more showers were scheduled for Saturdays at 1:00 P.M. After speaking with the Aides who came Saturday evenings, and being assured they had ample time to assist me with a shower in the evening, I became proactive and called and talked with two supervisors. I had every intention of talking to each supervisor's supervisor or director until I could get someone in authority to understand the situation. I did not have to go very far up the ladder. The end result was a shower scheduled for Saturday evenings. In my opinion, it is very upsetting when decisions are made by people who are not in touch with those who do the work. Once again, I received confirmation that I need to stand up for what I believe is right for me.

    The cooler weather of October was a reminder that winter would soon be upon us. I fervently hoped it would hold off for at least another month. The +10C degree temperatures were preferable to the freezing temperatures we experienced some years previously. I definitely did not spend as much time outdoors.

    I was feeling disappointed since it appeared I was not making much progress. October, 2021 has not been a month of huge improvements. I really needed Chris, the new physical therapist who took Nicole's place to show me what I was capable of. I showed him all I was doing and he did make a few changes. Instead of sidestepping down the ramp, he suggested I simply walk forward. This was a change I endorsed wholeheartedly. This was much easier and something I did normally. The huge change was doing squats at the towel bar in the bathroom. When he suggested I do this I could not believe it. However, when I stepped up to the bar, a feeling of calmness came over me. I knew I could do it. And I did just that. Of course, after four or five squats, I was wiped. However, after a rest I was ready for what-ever what came next. Side-stepping was next on the agenda. So now, I knew what the exercises would be when Home Care assisted me, squats followed by side stepping, followed by standing on my left foot and lifting my right so it barely touched the floor. Although the squats tired me out completely, it showed me that my legs and thighs were strengthened by doing all those sit-to-stands daily with Home Care. My next step forward will be squats holding on with one hand and then not holding on at all. I could do either but only one or two squats. It is necessary to do at least ten per set to increase strength and balance. Having seen some improvement, I am now content to work hard until I am able to accomplish ten squats without holding on.

An arm exercise was added. Sitting on the commode in the bathroom I would place my left arm on the vanity with my right. My Home Care Aide would hold it there for five to ten seconds while I held my right arm straight out beside me on the shower chair. If the Aide did not hold it in place, the left hand would slip off the cupboard. The objective was to help stretch the muscles so that spasticity would be alleviated and to bring back its range of motion.

The change in exercises reinforces the possibility of more improvement.

> "The struggle of life is one of our greatest blessings. It makes us patient, sensitive, and Godlike. It teaches us that although the world is full of suffering, it is also full of the overcoming of it."
> Helen Keller

Chapter 15
Family Perspective

No story is complete without hearing from Alvin and the rest of the family. This chapter is devoted to them.

Joslien woke me up at about 2:00 A.M. She was feeling strange and felt she should go to the hospital. I asked her if I could drive her or whether I should call the ambulance. As I was on the phone with the 911 operator her condition rapidly deteriorated. She had gotten dressed, then sat down and then lay on the bed. What was most alarming was she could not speak. The ambulance which is only fifteen minutes away in Tofield seemed to take hours. This was not unusual, when a GPS is used, it usually does not find our location, a person is directed north of Highway 14 instead of south. Eventually people realize they were misdirected and turn around.

I followed the ambulance with my car. I was grateful that the doctor was waiting in the Emergency Department when the ambulance and I arrived. The next few hours were a bit of a blur. I called both of our sons to let them know what had happened to their mom. At that point in time, it appeared there was no hope of Joslien surviving. Nursing staff asked when the stroke had occurred. I couldn't really give them an accurate time frame since the ambulance had taken so long to come. The decision was made not to give her TPA, a clot busting drug, which might have dissolved the stroke and lessened the severity of the symptoms.

Both boys arrived in the early morning. I called our daughter who lives in Lexington, Kentucky to let her know of the unfolding events.

I spent the next three months in limbo, not knowing if Joslien would live. In the first week I stayed overnight with her. I think it gave her comfort knowing I was there. Then hospital policies changed. I could not stay overnight but at least I could visit for a few hours during the day. When the Camrose Hospital called one day, I expected the worst. However, they had only called to say visitors were not allowed. I had brought the laptop in, so we were able to talk with each other via Facetime. Then, for a few weeks, on a week-end, Joslien, Lee and I would meet in the parking lot.

It was not until Joslien was transferred to Ponoka that I knew she would be okay. The progress was slow, but it was very evident. That she would get better, I was certain. I didn't even stop and consider how much she would improve, I just knew she was coming home to me eventually. When she was finally eating solid food about six months after the stroke, I knew that I had been right; it was only a matter of time before she was home. Several months later Joslien was transferred to Tofield and then home. It was very difficult in the early days. Although there was Home Care twice a day, I was not able to leave the house for more than one or two hours. I was her main caregiver. Once a week, Joslien had respite which would mean I could go to the city, run errands, etc. Respite was extra time allotted when Home Care was present to allow me to do what I needed to do without worrying about Joslien being alone.

Joslien has kept making progress. It is much easier for me. This summer I was able to leave for up to six hours to put up some hay. I have no doubt the progress will continue.

All three of our children were stunned when Joslien had her stroke. When several weeks had passed, they knew she would survive. Our son Alvin Jr. kept hoping she would improve enough to use her computer. Lee was possibly the most optimistic. Although he wasn't visualizing anything specific, he gave an apt analogy. "When a baby is born, it is helpless. A few months later it is able to sit up. Sometimes it takes up to eighteen months to walk. By two or three years of age it can run." Lee said "We don't know how much Mom will improve, but she will keep improving."

The following is from Laine's perspective.

"My brother, Lee, sent me a message in the early afternoon on a Sunday, saying simply, to call Dad. I then saw that my dad had called and left me two messages. I'm notorious for not checking my phone or turning the ringer back on in the morning. When I talked to my dad, he said Mom had a stroke and was in the hospital, and that she's ok; it took some time for me to get more information about what had happened and was happening. Everyone was in shock; which was understandable, and seemed unable to articulate what had happened. I had been living in Kentucky for a year at that time and being so far away from my parents was immediately very difficult at that moment. I felt helpless and this helplessness still persists. I was able to book a plane ticket for a day later, and arrange to start my new job a few days later than originally planned so I could come to Alberta, Canada for 5 days. Before I went into the hospital to see our Mom, my oldest brother, Alvin Gerald, tried to prepare me for what our Mom looked like - I assumed so I could be a strong support for her and not emotionally breakdown when I saw her and saw that she couldn't move (except her right arm just very slightly), she couldn't close her mouth or swallow, or speak (she only made noises for words). For those 5 days I tried to be a solid support for her before I had to fly right back to Kentucky.

    When I came back to Kentucky, I started my new job the next day. After the first week at my new job, Kentucky went into lock down for two months because of the Corona Virus. For the first few months or so after Mom had her stroke, I couldn't directly communicate with her and relied on updates from Dad. I would also call my Dad when he visited her so I could talk with my Mom even if I didn't fully understand what she was saying. Those first three months or so were very scary. There was at least a month where the hospital my Mom was at went into lock down and no one was allowed to visit her. There were so many uncertainties and unknowns. I thought, what if my Mom died? Would the borders be open for me to go to the funeral? Would I want to go with my Dad being in his 70's and possibly bringing the Corona Virus to him and the rest of my family that is already devastated? How would my Dad cope? My Mom got better over time; it definitely wasn't immediate in any sense of the word, but she did improve and is still improving. I am so happy she's still on this earth and able to do some of the things she was able to do before. It has been over a year since her stroke and I am finally starting to plan a trip to visit her and the rest of my family next year."

    When I read Laine's perspective I was stunned. I had never considered or spent much time on wondering how my family was coping. I was so totally immersed in dealing with my stroke I was oblivious to what they were going through. And perhaps this was meant to be this way.

My energy needed to be directed towards healing myself first.

Since I have come home, I am very aware of how much my family cares. I am particularly cognizant of how much time and energy my husband Alvin puts into helping me. If it was not for his awesome care and attention, I would not be doing as good as I am.

"Today is the blocks with which we build."
Henry Wadsworth Longfellow

Chapter 16
Dawn Of A New Day

I am grateful to be alive, to see my great-granddaughter's smile, to watch my youngest granddaughter play on the varsity basketball team in high school, to watch while two granddaughters become the excellent teachers I know they will be, to see my oldest granddaughter be an outstanding heavy duty equipment technician. It is satisfying to know my children are happy and doing well in their career choices. All of their significant others are beautiful and caring, both inside and out.

About the middle of October, I was given evidence that I was definitely improving. Up until this time, I used a sock on my left shoe as a slider. I could easily step forward with my right foot but my left would drag. The slider would enable me to drag my left foot forward. When Chris, my physical therapist, asked me to walk, I did so, without a sock being placed on my left shoe to use as a slider. This time I was able to lift the left foot a tiny amount, enough that I was able to walk with the help of my cane. I was extremely happy.

Another development occurred a few weeks later. Alvin and I went into the city to do some shopping. I was able to get into the car without help. When we arrived in the city, I was able to get out of the car without any help. The next store we went to, I repeated getting in and out again once more just to prove to myself I could do it. Once more I had a glimmer of hope I would one day get into the vehicle and go to town by myself. I will regain my independence.

Sandra Dee continues to come once a week. She has me side-stepping at the railing, walking up and down the ramp, and standing and balancing on my left foot. My progress is more evident to her since she only sees me once every week. Instead of wearing my foot brace, I now wear a device called a foot flexor. It goes around my ankle and attaches to the shoelaces of my runner. As a result, my toes are pulled up slightly. This enables me to walk without the slider even when I am tired.

Since I had vacuumed my SUV one or two months earlier, I decided it was time to do the same with our car. This was more of a challenge. Our car is much lower to the ground, so I needed to bend over much further. It definitely challenged my sense of balance. I was able to accomplish most of what I wanted to do, then I felt the rear seat area needed more work. In order to reach all the nooks and crannies, I moved from my wheelchair to the back seat. It was so much easier to vacuum from here. The problem was, I could not get out when I was finished. In the front, there is a loop on the top of the door frame which helps me to leverage my body out. In the back, there is no loop. I attempted to stand up without hitting my head on the frame of the roof of the car. After several attempts I checked the time on my phone. It would be forty-five minutes before Home Care arrived to help with evening care. Sitting and waiting is not something I like to do. Another option was calling Alvin for assistance since I had my phone. However, this would mean interrupting his work. I decided not to bother him. My third option was getting out of the car myself. Luckily, I had my electric wheelchair. I was able to reach the controls and maneuvered it closer, then farther from the door. At last I had it in the perfect position where I was able to reach the arm rest and pull myself up and out of the car. The whole ordeal took me a half an hour. In hindsight, I could have just waited an extra fifteen minutes for assistance from Home Care, but I would not have had the satisfaction of accomplishing the task myself.

    The electric wheelchair is not used inside the house. Anyone with mechanical experience knows there is no forgiveness or understanding with machines. When the forward gear is pushed, the chair goes forward regardless of whether or not body parts are in the way. So, knees, hands or toes need to be safely out of harm's way. Similarly, an electric wheelchair will run into a wall if the operator is not careful. Because I do not wish my house walls to be damaged, and because I prefer to force my left hand to work even though it is difficult, the electric chair is saved for outdoor excursions only.

    November brought cooler temperatures and snow which is not unexpected in our part of the northern hemisphere. The snow does hamper our outdoor excursions. As I learned the previous winter, snow on streets makes outdoor expeditions much more difficult. On a trip to Costco, after shopping with their motorized cart/scooter my husband and I decided to take our groceries to our car which was parked nearby in a handicapped stall. Their motorized scooter did a lot of spinning on the snow-covered pavement of the parking lot. Alvin had to assist me by pushing the scooter. Later the two of us laughed at the picture we must have presented to others. It did teach us a valuable lesson. Next time we will park beside the doors in the no parking zone which a lot of people ignore anyway. Alvin will get their motorized scooter, assist me in getting seated and then park the car. When we have completed our shopping, the procedure will be repeated only in reverse.

December heralded the arrival of frigid temperatures. On December sixteenth our temperature near Edmonton, Alberta was -29°C. Twenty-one months after my stroke, there are still small improvements. Chris had started me doing squats at the towel bar; first holding on with both hands, then progressing to holding on with one hand. I am now able to perform two sets of five squats without holding on at all. Then since I am tired and because holding on is easier, I do ten squats in the last set. It is my intent to be ale to do three sets of ten squats without holding on.

In addition, I do exercises using a pulley system hooked onto my bedroom door. I sit in my wheelchair and push down with my right hand and arm. The purpose is to increase the range of motion of my left arm. After two weeks I progressed to doing one set of ten of these exercises standing up. Standing up assists me in regaining balance. Because this is tiring, I sit down to do another two sets of ten.

This whole stroke experience has taught me several important lessons or virtues. The first is gratitude. Be grateful for everything. When life appears bleak, look for tiny things to be grateful for, a tissue, a visitor, your phone or a smile on someone's face. When you are grateful, life in turn smiles upon you and gives you more to be grateful for. Or, as you may have heard the saying, "what you give out comes back to you." Karma is another word that I believe could be used.

The second is patience. This does not mean just sitting back and expecting things to happen. Patience and hard work, the third virtue, work well together. Know that you will improve, work hard and it will happen.

Being kind and gentle with yourself are important. There are ups and downs in life, particularly in stroke recovery. Rejoice in the ups, know the downs are temporary. You will get through it.

Have goals in mind. I had one major goal, to walk. To me, the other little goal such as toileting unassisted would happen once I could walk. I was right. Now that I can walk a very short distance with a quad cane, I am setting new and different goals. I plan on walking without a cane. I also plan on driving into town myself. So, if you need to set small goals for yourself, do so. Or, if like me, one huge goal may be all you need. Set your goal then focus, and work towards it. I never doubted I would walk. Thankfully everyone around me supported me and never openly suggested I would not be able to do this. All these major goals can be applied to life in general. There are many "new-age" proponents who advocate goal setting. I am very happy about this. However, without working towards the goals, nothing much may happen.

Finally, the last (or some people would say first) necessary element is prayer. Many people will find comfort in prayer. I had many people praying for me. Some prayed to God, others prayed to the Creator. Still others asked the Universe or a Higher Power. Prayer is powerful but I believe in the old adage "God helps those who help themselves!" Prayer combined with hard work yields the best results.

The common thread that runs through these required components is hard work. Of course, this also applies to life in general. The people who are driven to succeed work their butts off!

It is now December 2021, twenty-one months post stroke. I still have zoom group sessions with my speech therapist. Another participant mentioned that she had stayed at a special rehab facility for an entire year. At one point in time her wheelchair was taken away from her and she was forced to walk. This gave me an idea. I would refuse to use the chair except for early mornings when I knew from experience that I was extremely unsteady. This worked well for three days. Then the fourth and fifth day, my body refused to cooperate. Even my right foot seemed to hesitate; I had a difficult time moving it forward. I was only able to do short trips to the bathroom. Thankfully I had Sandra Dee come and do some therapy with me. The temperature was 0 degrees C (+32F). We bundled up, went outside and since Alvin had cleared the snow off the deck, I was able to sidestep and also walk holding onto the railing. The fresh air did wonders. I was not up to the level of my previous accomplishments, but I was satisfied with what I had done. I continue to use the wheelchair less often but I do not push my body to the point of exhaustion. I push it until it's tired, then stop and rest, and then push it again. In the early mornings I do not push it at all. Since I am too unsteady to walk, instead of risking a fall I allow my husband to propel me to the table. Then after fifteen minutes or so, after my first coffee, I feel I am ready to push my body as far as it will go. I do not have anyone to push me, to guide me to attempt new ventures, so it is up to me to force my body to respond to my wishes.

    A stroke is devastating. It robs you of many things you could do for yourself. If you allow yourself to feel defeated, you will be. You can give up and dwell on how unfair life is. Or like me, you can choose to fight back. You are a survivor, a warrior.

About The Author

Joslien lives with her husband on an acreage near Ryley, Alberta. Prior to 2020 she led an active life, teaching First Aid classes and compiling a family history book as well as doing all the yard work. She compiled a 384 page volume on her husband's family entitled Peter and Maria Wanechko - Their Legacy. Another of her accomplishments involved writing a series of herbal articles for a local newspaper as well as writing articles on different healing practises she does for a different publication.

Joslien loves adventure and has travelled to many places; she incorporated this love with her passion for learning. She has had many teachers and mentors. A trip to Thailand was taken with her daughter during the early days of self-discovery with her teacher Laung Phor Viriyang Sirintaro, a Buddist monk. Three days of the fourteen were spent trekking up Mount Doi Inthanon with meditation every morning and evening. Her trip to Japan included a hike up Mount Kurama with her sensi Hyukaten Inamoto. A trip to India with a yoga group included the company of Kushok, a Buddhist monk and a student of the Dalai Lama. These three teachers, as well as others here at home, have influenced the way she dealt with the challenges she faced. Thankfully her husband enjoys to travel as much as she does and happily accompanies her. They love checking out different massage places together as well as enjoying the different cultures. Both of them often go off the resorts to meet locals and come home with a greater appreciation of life in Alberta, Canada.

In March 2020, she had a major stroke. This book recounts her resilient journey to recovery.

www.ingramcontent.com/pod-product-compliance
Lightning Source LLC
LaVergne TN
LVHW051510070426
835507LV00022B/3026